Does God Want Me Well?

Discovery Series Bible Study

Does God use sickness in the lives of His children to build character? Is this consistent with the actions of a loving God? Are we sick because we don't have the faith to be healed? Is God healing people today through the ministry of faith healers? When sickness or suffering attacks us or someone close to us, what should we think? What should we do?

These questions, and many others like them, are answered in this booklet by RBC senior research editor Herb Vander Lugt. He shows what the Bible teaches about healing. And he uncovers four positive, unassailable certainties that every child of God can count on in times of sickness and suffering.

Martin R. De Haan II, President of RBC Ministries

Publisher:	Discovery House Publishers
Editor:	David Sper
Graphic Design:	Alex Soh, Janet Chim, Felix Xu
Cover Photo:	Alex Soh © 2001 RBC Ministries Asia Ltd.
Series Coordinator/Study Guide:	Bill Crowder, Sim Kay Tee

This *Discovery Series Bible Study* is based on the *Discovery Series* booklet *"Does God Want Me Well?"* (Q0104) from RBC Ministries. The *Discovery Series* has more than 140 titles on a variety of biblical and Christian-living issues. These 32-page booklets offer a rich resource of insight for your study of God's Word.
For a catalog of *Discovery Series* booklets, write to
RBC Ministries, PO Box 2222, Grand Rapids, MI 49501-2222
or visit us on the Web at: www.discoveryseries.org

 **Discovery House Publishers**

A member of the RBC Ministries family:
Our Daily Bread, Day Of Discovery, RBC Radio, Discovery Series, Campus Journal, Discovery House Music, Sports Spectrum

ISBN 1-57293-095-0

Table Of Contents

The Problem Of Pain

The man responded angrily to my attempts to help. He was dying of lung cance and was full of bitterness. He told me he didn't want to hear about a God wh lets people suffer the way they do. He said, "I turned against the Bible and th Christian faith when my mother was dying of the same disease I have. She was devout Christian, but in spite of her prayers that God would either heal her c take her home, she lived with terrible pain month after month. I decided tha either there isn't a God or that He isn't the kind of God you think He is."

Many people turn away from God because of the problem of pain.

My heart went out to him, but nothing I said made an impression on him Finally I asked, "Did your mother turn away from God too?" He responded, "Nc she kept talking about God's grace and about going to be with Jesus." Then h quickly added, "But I don't have the kind of faith she had."

Without question, many people turn away from God because of th problem of pain. They find it hard to believe that a loving and all-powerful Go would permit good people to suffer the way they do. On the other hanc thousands have testified that it was during a time of deep sorrow or intens anguish that they found God more real and precious than ever before.

Christians
Agree And Disagree

As Christians, we agree that God is loving, wise, and all-powerful. We agree that this good God gave His moral creatures freedom to choose between good and evil, and that their wrong choice brought His curse upon the earth. We also agree that this infinitely wise and good God is working out a program for our ultimate good and His glory.

However, even among us who believe the Bible, there are a few areas of disagreement. We give different answers to two very important questions, one having to do with the purpose of pain and the other with the matter of supernatural healing.

Does God use sickness to make good people better?

Ken Blue, an evangelical Christian with an effective ministry in Vancouver, says no. He writes:

> What we would call abuse in a human family, some have labeled a blessing in the family of God. Francis McNutt explains, "What human father or mother would choose cancer for their daughter to tame her pride?" . . . One of the greatest hindrances to a vital healing ministry in the church today is the notion that sickness is essentially good for us, that it is sent to purify the soul and build character (*Authority To Heal*, InterVarsity Press, pp.21-22).

On the other hand, Dr. M. R. De Haan, physician, minister, and founder of Radio Bible Class, said that God does use sickness in the lives of His children to make them better. He wrote:

> The greatest sermons I have ever heard were not preached from pulpits, but from sickbeds. The greatest, deepest truths of God's Word have often been revealed . . . by humble souls who have gone through the seminary of affliction and have learned experientially the deep things of the ways of God.

**"Grapes must be crushed
before wine can be made.
Wheat must be broken
to make bread." — M. R. De Haan**

Are you afflicted and suffering, precious child of God? Then remember—your Father still knows best. . . . Grapes must be crushed before wine can be made. Unless the violin is stretched until it cries out in pain, there is no music in it. Wheat must be broken to make bread. We may not know what God is doing now, but someday we shall understand and be like Him (*Broken Things*, Discovery House Publishers, 1988, pp.44,91).

Is God working obvious miracles of healing today?

Dr. William Noland, after a period of diligent research, declared that he found no evidence that God is working miraculous healings or that He has given any person the gift to do so. He writes:

> Two years ago I began looking for a healing miracle. When I started my search, I hoped to find some evidence that someone, somewhere, had supernatural powers that he or she would employ to cure those patients we doctors, with all our knowledge and training, must still label as "incurable." As I have said before, I have been unable to find any such miracle worker (*Healing: A Doctor In Search Of A Miracle*, Fawcett, 1967, p.272).

Dr. J. Sidlow Baxter, a well-known Bible teacher, says yes. He writes:

The fact that many wonderful miracle healings are occurring today in great public healing rallies, who can deny? Only those deny who have not been and seen. With my own eyes almost jumping out of their sockets, I have seen the dumb from birth given speech, the stone-deaf given new hearing, the long blind suddenly given new vision, terminal cancer instantaneously cured (and later medically attested), crippled arthritics released and straightened on the spot, wheelchair victims of multiple sclerosis wheel their own chairs away, not to mention other such wonderful healings (*Divine Healing Of The Body*, Zondervan, 1979, p.270).

We can answer both of these questions with a solid yes. God does use suffering as a means of our spiritual advancement. Moreover, He does heal miraculously—but not always. And when He doesn't, we need not blame ourselves or give in to despair.

God does heal miraculously—but not always. And when He doesn't, we need not blame ourselves or give in to despair.

STUDY NO. **1**

Understanding The Problem

Job 2:10—"[Job] said to her, 'You speak as one of the foolish women speaks. Shall we indeed accept good from God, and shall we not accept adversity?' In all this Job did not sin with his lips."

Objective:
To understand how our response to the issue of healing can affect our understanding of God and His purposes.

Bible Memorization:
Job 2:10

Reading:
"The Problem Of Pain" & "Christians Agree & Disagree" pp.4-7

Warming Up
Have you ever known someone who prayed for physical healing but was not healed? How did that person respond to the lack of healing? How would you respond?

Thinking Through
Consider this statement from page 4: "Without question, many people turn away from God because of the problem of pain." Why would pain cause people to turn away from God? Can pain bring about other responses? What are some?

On page 6, Dr. M. R. De Haan is quoted as saying, "The greatest sermons I have ever heard were not preached from pulpits, but from sickbeds." What enables people to respond so positively to deep suffering?

According to pages 5-7, on what two important questions about healing do Christians disagree? What is the root of that disagreement? How would you answer each question?

Digging In
Key Text: 2 Corinthians 12:1-10
How had Paul's "thorn" affected his life and his relationship with God? How could Paul say that his sickness was a gift from God and at the same time "a messenger of Satan"? (v.7).

Why would Paul "boast" only about his illness and the lack of healing in his life when he could have boasted of the many spectacular and miraculous experiences he had enjoyed? In what ways is Paul different from some modern healers today?

Why didn't God heal Paul? (2 Cor. 12:7-10). How was the grace of God sufficient for him? What did Paul mean when he said, "I take pleasure in infirmities, in reproaches, in needs, in persecutions, in distresses, for Christ's sake. For when I am weak, then I am strong"? (v.10).

Going Further
Refer
In Romans 8:28, Paul did not say that "all things *are* good." Rather he said, "all things *work together for* good." Why is this distinction important? Does "all things" include sickness, ill health, pain, and suffering? How do "all things work together for good"?

Reflect
Have there been times when you have personally struggled with the problem of pain? As you begin this study, commit your heart to allowing God to bring you an understanding of His purposes, promises, and love for you—in spite of past disappointments.

"7Lest I should be exalted above measure by the abundance of the revelations, a thorn in the flesh was given to me, a messenger of Satan to buffet me, lest I be exalted above measure. 8Concerning this thing I pleaded with the Lord three times that it might depart from me. 9And He said to me, 'My grace is sufficient for you, for My strength is made perfect in weakness.' Therefore most gladly I will rather boast in my infirmities, that the power of Christ may rest upon me. 10Therefore I take pleasure in infirmities, in reproaches, in needs, in persecutions, in distresses, for Christ's sake. For when I am weak, then I am strong."
2 Corinthians 12:7-10

Biblical Certainties

She was a nurse and was quite sure she knew what she had. Yet her face blanched when the doctor came into the hospital room and said, "Sue, I hate to tell you what you already suspect is true. You have multiple sclerosis." She was aware of what she would be enduring—gradual paralysis, speech problems, impaired vision, jerking muscle tremors, and probably times of intense pain. It was not a pleasant prospect.

After the doctor left, Sue and her husband cried, but not for long. They prayed, talked to each other, and expressed their faith. As a result, they both sensed the presence of the Holy Spirit. They received strength to go on. Now, some 20 years later, they are doing quite well. The disease has progressed, but far more slowly than expected.

The essential elements of this scenario are occurring all the time. No family escapes completely unscathed. Not many, even among the most godly, enjoy excellent health until old age and slip quietly off into the next world. It just doesn't work out that way. That is why we need to know what the Bible teaches about sickness and healing.

The following study will uncover four positive, unassailable certainties that every child of God can count on in times of sickness and suffering:

1. God will make you well.
2. God hurts when you hurt.
3. God knows why you're suffering.
4. God is in control.

God Will Make You Well

If you are a sick or suffering Christian, you can stand on the certainty that God will make you well—perhaps on earth, but surely in heaven. That's His guarantee. As His children, we are destined to receive a new, glorified body and to live forever in heaven. The apostle Paul drew tremendous comfort from his expectation of resurrection and eternal glory. After reaffirming the fact of Christ's resurrection in 1 Corinthians 15, he proceeded to point out that we too will receive resurrection bodies like the one Christ has (vv.20-58). This truth sustained him as he suffered in his service for the Lord. In a spirit of joy and optimism he wrote:

> *Therefore we do not lose heart. Even though our outward man is perishing, yet the inward man is being renewed day by day. For our light affliction, which is but for a moment, is working for us a far more exceeding and eternal weight of glory, while we do not look at the things which are seen, but at the things which are not seen. For the things which are seen are temporary, but the things which are not seen are eternal. For we know that if our earthly house, this tent, is destroyed, we have a building from God, a house not made with hands, eternal in the heavens (2 Cor. 4:16–5:1).*

Maybe you don't react to these words with much enthusiasm. You want healing in the here and now. Your feelings are not unusual. Suffering is not pleasant. We instinctively want good health and freedom from pain. We want it now. But when we let ourselves think this way, we are looking at life from the vantage point of those who have no real hope of heaven, those who tell us to grab all the gusto we can because "we only go around once."

That's wrong! Believers in Christ should live above the merely human level. We are to face squarely the fact that this life is brief at best and that things down here are never perfect. We are called on to exercise our faith and to look beyond the immediate and earthly. We will live forever in a wonderful new world! When we really grasp this truth, we can share the victorious attitude expressed by Paul in 2 Corinthians 4. We will begin to anticipate joyously the unseen and eternal realities of heaven. Indeed, we will "rejoice in hope of the glory of God" (Rom. 5:2).

Joel A. Freeman gives us an example of a person who learned to do this. He writes:

Brian understands this principle. He has learned it the hard way. His 18-year-old eyes communicate mischief as he tries to run over my toes with his souped-up electric wheelchair. (Remind me to wear my steel-toed boots next time I visit him.) Four years ago Brian was riding his 10-speed bicycle when a drunken driver careened across the median strip and hit him broadside. Brian pitched head over heels for 30 yards. The next thing he remembered was the soft touch of a nurse's hand on his forehead— 5 days later. As a paraplegic, Brian has battled the icy grip of self-pity. He's grappled with the seductive whisper of suicide. But you know what? He has won a tremendous victory—he has accepted God's sovereignty in the whole matter. Brian's physical condition has made marginal improvements. His attitude, however, has made a 180-degree turn, from cyclical bouts with rage and hopelessness to sparkling eyes filled with an eternal purpose for living. He has become a 'wounded healer' comforting others wherein he has been comforted" (*God Is Not Fair*, Here's Life Publishers, p.110).

No, Brian is not completely well physically. But he has experienced God's presence. He knows he is a member of that great body of suffering saints who have gone before (Heb. 11:30–12:4). This encourages him and makes him eager for the day when he will be completely well and with them.

God Hurts When You Hurt

If you are a suffering believer, the second biblical certainty from which you can draw great strength is the knowledge that God is suffering with you. He is not the "unmoved Mover" of Greek philosophy. He is not an unfeeling Being oblivious to the pain of His creatures. On the contrary, He is our loving heavenly Father. He hurts when we hurt. The psalmist declared, "As a father pities his children, so the Lord pities those who fear Him. For He knows our frame; He remembers that we are dust" (Ps. 103:13-14).

In reviewing God's dealings with Israel, the prophet wrote, "In all their affliction He was afflicted . . . ; in His love and in His pity He redeemed them" (Isa. 63:9). The Old Testament prophets repeatedly pictured God as delighting in blessing His children and as grieving when they must suffer.

The truth that God hurts when we hurt did not find full expression however, until it was revealed in the person of Jesus Christ. He is Immanuel, "God with us" (Isa. 7:14). He, the Second Person of the eternal Trinity, became a member of our humanity. He suffered everything we can suffer. He was born in a stable, a member of a poor family. He grew up in a humble home in a small village. He worked as a laboring man until He was 30. He didn't have a home during His 3 years of ministry. He was resented by His half brothers. He was rejected by the Jewish people to whom He came. He was misunderstood and misrepresented. He was mocked. He was falsely accused. He was betrayed by a close companion. He was forsaken by His closest friends. He was scourged. He was forced to carry a heavy wooden beam on His lacerated back. He was nailed to a cross. And even as He hung on it, He endured the taunts of mockers.

Why did He do all this? Couldn't He have paid the price for our sins without going through all of this humiliation and abuse? As far as we know, the answer is yes. His death on the cross, not his pre-Calvary suffering, atoned for our sin. It seems that He underwent all this added pain and humiliation for two reasons: to reveal God's heart (2 Cor. 4:6), and to become our sympathetic high priest (Heb. 4:15-16). God had always hurt when His people hurt. But He did so in a real, tangible manner through the incarnation—through the event that began in Bethlehem.

> **The truth that God hurts when we hurt**
> **did not find full expression until it was revealed**
> **in the person of Jesus Christ.**

Are you suffering? Are you grieving? Are you disappointed because you are going to die before you can realize your plans and hopes? Be assured that God cares. He hurts with you. He doesn't like what you are enduring any more than you do. He could intervene and heal you instantly. But if He were to do this for you and every other person who is suffering, no one would have a need for the kind of faith that builds Christian character. Therefore, He allows you to suffer. But all the while He, like you, is looking forward to the time when all human pain will be over.

J. I. Packer has stated this truth eloquently:

God's love to sinners involves His identifying Himself with their needs. Such an identification is involved in all love: it is indeed the test of whether love is genuine or not . . . . It is not for nothing that the Bible habitually speaks of God as the loving Father and Husband of His people. It follows from the very nature of these relationships that God's happiness will not be complete till all His beloved ones are finally out of trouble . . . . He has in effect resolved that henceforth for all eternity His happiness shall be conditional upon ours. Thus God saves not only for His glory, but for His gladness (*Knowing God*, InterVarsity Press, 1973, p.113).

Just as a good husband suffers when he sees his wife in pain, and loving parents feel the distress of their children, so also the Lord hurts when you hurt. And He won't be completely happy until you hurt no more.

⚜
STUDY
NO. 2

Biblical Certainties

God Heals & God Hurts

2 Corinthians 4:16—
"Therefore we do not lose heart. Even though our outward man is perishing, yet the inward man is being renewed day by day."

Objective:
To embrace two of four certainties that every child of God can count on in times of sickness and suffering.

Bible Memorization:
2 Corinthians 4:16

Reading:
**"Biblical Certainties,"
"God Will Make You Well," & "God Hurts When You Hurt"
pp.11-15**

Warming Up
What are some of the uncertainties we go through during times of sickness and suffering? What are the different ways we respond to them?

Thinking Through
On page 11 the statement is made, "Not many, even among the most godly, enjoy excellent health until old age and slip quietly off into the next world. It just doesn't work out that way." Do you agree? If so, why are we often so unprepared for ill health to be part of our experience?

We are told that thoughts of healing in heaven don't always cause people to "react to these words with much enthusiasm. You want healing in the here and now" (p.12). Do you view that kind of hope as encouraging or empty? Why?

On page 14 we are challenged to think of God as One who hurts when we hurt (Isa. 63:9). How does God suffer with us, hurting when we hurt? What are some ways that this idea can bring comfort to a person struggling with pain and illness?

Digging In
Key Text: 2 Corinthians 4:16–5:1

What did Paul mean when he said that "our outward man is perishing, yet the inward man is being renewed day by day"? (v.16).

How did the truths of verses 16-18 help Paul cope with his suffering and trials? What does this passage say to the view that we should expect to be healed here and now?

How does 2 Corinthians 5:1 describe the body in which you will enjoy eternity? How does this verse affirm that God will heal us ultimately? What hope does this give us in times of pain now?

Going Further
Refer

According to Hebrews 2:17-18 and 4:15 16, what did Jesus do to show us that God suffers with us when we suffer?

Reflect

In what ways has prayer helped you cope when you are ill? When have you prayed, "Lord, heal me!" and when have you been able to pray, "Lord, Your will be done"?

"¹⁶Therefore we do not lose heart. Even though our outward man is perishing, yet the inward man is being renewed day by day. ¹⁷For our light affliction, which is but for a moment, is working for us a far more exceeding and eternal weight of glory, ¹⁸while we do not look at the things which are seen, but at the things which are not seen. For the things which are seen are temporary, but the things which are not seen are eternal. ¹For we know that if our earthly house, this tent, is destroyed, we have a building from God, a house not made with hands, eternal in the heavens."

2 Corinthians 4:16–5:1

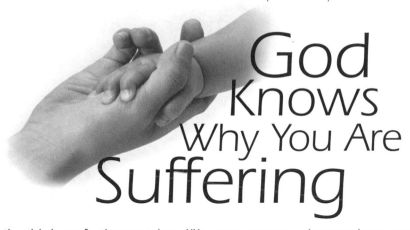

God Knows Why You Are Suffering

This is the third comforting certainty. We want answers when we hurt, so we cry out, "Why?" God's special servants may even do this when grief or pain comes their way.

I know a minister who recently learned he had cancer. He was displeased with God's ways. He told a friend, "I can't understand why God let this happen to me. I've served Him faithfully. I'm not nurturing a secret sin. I've taken care of my body: I eat healthful foods. I avoid sweets, coffee, and soda pop. I keep my weight under control. I don't think I deserve this."

His protests remind us of those raised by Job almost 4,000 years ago. He hurled out the word *why* a total of 16 times. He even listed 12 ways in which he had been a moral, honest, kind, and loving man (Job 31:1-14). But God never answered Job's why questions. Nor did He answer this query as it came from the lips of my minister friend. However, God did something better. He gave them the assurance that He knew why. He did so by reminding them of the great wisdom and power He displayed in His creation of the world. Moreover, He brought both of them to the place where they acknowledged His ways to be perfect in wisdom and goodness.

Sometimes we *can* answer the question "Why?" It is always good to search our hearts to see if we bear some blame for our pain. We may be sick because we have not obeyed common-sense rules of health. Maybe the accident that hurt us is the result of our carelessness. It is also possible that our illness is the result of

God's chastening because of sin in our lives (1 Cor. 11:29-30; Heb. 12:6). The Bible teaches us that some Christians die an untimely death (humanly speaking) because of sin (Acts 5:1-11; 1 Cor. 11:30). If we know we have been living disobediently, we must repent. God may give us healing when we do. And when we see the death of a believing loved one who has fallen into sinful ways, we can take comfort in the assurance that God sometimes takes one of His children home rather than see him continue on his destructive course.

However, we often can't find specific answers to our why questions. We can't always expect to know the reason why we are suffering. But even then, God does not leave us completely in the dark. In addition to assuring us that He knows why, He has shown us that even unexplained suffering has a valuable purpose.

In John 9, Jesus used an encounter with a blind man to teach His disciples this lesson. They asked Him, "Rabbi, who sinned, this man or his parents, that he was born blind?" (v.2). They obviously saw this affliction as punishment for somebody's sin—either that of his parents or himself while he was still in the womb. Jesus answered them, "Neither this man nor his parents sinned, but that the works of God should be revealed in him" (v.3). This man's affliction was not punishment for any special sin. But it had value. It was designed to make him the vehicle through which God's power could be put on display. After He had made this point, Jesus said, "I must work the works of Him who sent Me while it is day; the night is coming when no one can work" (v.4). Then He gave the man his sight.

The application to us is obvious. Instead of wasting our energy in useless speculation about the why question, let's view suffering—our own or that which we encounter in others—as an opportunity to demonstrate God's power and bring glory to Him. Maybe He will answer our prayers by healing us. Perhaps He will use the suffering of someone we love to make us more compassionate, more kind, more helpful. Or He may let us suffer, but give us such supernatural grace that we will be a vibrant testimony to His glory. Actually, God has many good reasons for letting us suffer:

- Suffering silences Satan (Job 1–2).
- Suffering gives God an opportunity to be glorified (Jn. 11:4).
- Suffering makes us more like Christ (Phil. 3:10; Heb. 2:10).
- Suffering makes us appreciative (Rom. 8:28).

- Suffering teaches us to depend on God (Ex. 14:13-14; Isa. 40:28-31).
- Suffering enables us to exercise our faith (Job 23:10; Rom. 8:24-25).
- Suffering teaches us patience (Rom. 5:3; Jas. 1:2-4).
- Suffering makes us sympathetic (2 Cor. 1:3-6).
- Suffering makes and keeps us humble (2 Cor. 12:7-10).
- Suffering brings rewards (2 Tim. 2:12; 1 Pet. 4:12-13).

Many other reasons for suffering could be given. We may not know which one fits our situation, but God does. That's comforting.

Instead of wasting our energy in useless speculation about the why question, let's view suffering— our own or that which we encounter in others— as an opportunity to demonstrate God's power and bring glory to Him.

God Is In Control

This is the fourth biblical certainty for suffering believers. The fact that God is in control doesn't mean that He is the direct cause of every injury or disease. They sometimes come through Satan and usually through the outworking of natural laws that God has built into the universe.

Satan was the one who robbed Job of his possessions, children, and health. The woman Jesus healed from a crippling illness was "a daughter of Abraham, whom Satan has bound . . . for eighteen years" (Lk. 13:16). Satan was also involved in the "destruction of the flesh" in a disciplined church member (1 Cor. 5:5). And Paul's "thorn in the flesh" was a "messenger of Satan to buffet" him (2 Cor. 12:7).

> **Jesus assured us that nothing can happen to us unless it passes God's permissive will.**

Most suffering, however, is the result of natural processes. Habitual drunkenness leads to hallucinations, slurred speech, and physical collapse (Prov. 23:29-35). The young man entering the house of a prostitute is like an ox going into the slaughterhouse (Prov. 7:22). Timothy's stomach problems were probably related to the water he drank (1 Tim. 5:23). Many illnesses are eliminated through inoculations, diet, and good health habits. It's obvious that we cannot make God the primary agent in a large percentage of the suffering that plagues mankind.

The fact that Satan and natural factors are the direct agents in much human suffering, however, should not be taken as evidence that God is not involved.

These evils would not have occurred if He hadn't permitted them. God gave the devil permission to afflict Job, but He set the limits (Job 1–2). Even when accidents or illness can be traced to human carelessness or natural causes, they occur because God allows them. Jesus assured us that nothing can happen to us unless it passes God's permissive will. He said that even a seemingly insignificant event like the death of a sparrow does not occur "apart from your Father's will" (Mt. 10:29). Paul expressed God's control of everything by declaring that we who believe are "predestined according to the purpose of Him who works all things according to the counsel of His will" (Eph. 1:11).

The perfectly wise and good God you serve has everything under control. He has your ultimate welfare in view.

God has everything under His control. He may allow the devil to test you by making you sick. He may permit you to suffer great pain through an accident caused by carelessness or through a vicious attack by an evil person. These unpleasant events try us and may even tempt us to sin, but we can rest in the following assurance:

> No temptation [test] has overtaken you except such as is common to man; but God is faithful, who will not allow you to be tempted beyond what you are able, but with the temptation will also make the way of escape, that you may be able to bear it (1 Cor. 10:13).

No matter what your trial, no matter how great your pain or grief, remember that it passed the permissive will of your heavenly Father before it reached you. He loves you. He may heal you miraculously. If not, He will be with you in all your pain and someday take you to heaven. No matter what He does, He has your ultimate welfare in view. The perfectly wise and good God you serve has everything under control.

STUDY NO. 3

Biblical Certainties
God Knows & God Controls

Romans 8:28—"We know that all things work together for good to those who love God, to those who are the called according to His purpose."

Objective:

To embrace the third and fourth of four certainties that every child of God can count on in times of sickness and suffering.

Bible Memorization:
Romans 8:28

Reading:
"God Knows Why You Are Suffering" & "God Is In Control" pp.19-23

Warming Up
How can you reconcile the statement on page 23 that the "perfectly wise and good God you serve has everything under control" with the apparent chaos and turmoil that plagues our world?

Thinking Through
Sometimes we have to take some of the blame for our sickness or suffering. What examples of this are given on pages 19-20? Why is it difficult for us to consider how we may have contributed to our own suffering?

What are the 10 significant reasons that God might allow us to suffer? (see pp.20-21). Which is the easiest for you to accept? Which is the most difficult? In each case, why do you feel that way?

If everything is under God's control (pp.22-23), what elements of Satan's participation in our suffering are brought into clearer focus for you? Which elements are made more difficult for you personally to grasp?

24

Digging In
Key Text: John 9:1-5

What is troubling about the disciples' response to the blind man's condition? (v.2). What's inappropriate about always trying to fix blame for the troubles we face?

In these verses, Jesus spoke of His mission. What did He say was the real purpose for the man's affliction? How did His statement (v.3) counteract the disciples' assumption that the blind man's condition was rooted in a specific act of sin?

Why was the healing of the man's blindness appropriate for displaying Jesus as "the Light of the world"? How does the idea of physical sight relate to the spiritual realm?

Going Further
Refer

Compare Jesus' description of the cause of the man's blindness in John 9 with Paul's response to his thorn in the flesh in 2 Corinthians 12. How are the two events similar? How are they different?

Reflect

The truth that everything is under God's control can sometimes be overwhelming. Identify the areas in your own life where you struggle to acknowledge His control. Ask the Holy Spirit to enable you to confidently trust God to bring good out of "all things" (Rom. 8:28).

"¹Now as Jesus passed by, He saw a man who was blind from birth. ²And His disciples asked Him, saying, 'Rabbi, who sinned, this man or his parents, that he was born blind?' ³Jesus answered, 'Neither this man nor his parents sinned, but that the works of God should be revealed in him. ⁴I must work the works of Him who sent Me while it is day; the night is coming when no one can work. ⁵As long as I am in the world, I am the light of the world.'"
John 9:1-5

EXPLORING THE SCRIPTURES

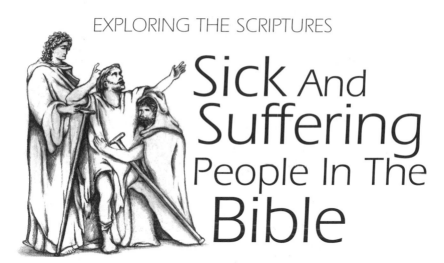

Sick And Suffering People In The Bible

The Bible gives us many accounts of severe illness, intense suffering, deep sorrow, and untimely death. These things are either attributed to God or to Satan. And on some occasions the source is not given. Sometimes healing came through a miracle. At other times, it came through a natural cure. And on some occasions, temporal healing didn't come at all—the person died. Sometimes the reason is stated. At other times it is implied. And on some occasions it is not indicated in any way.

Job (Job 1–42)

- Identity—a godly and wealthy man who lived some 4,000 years ago (1:1-5).
- Affliction—loss of property, death of children, painful skin disease (1:13-19; 2:1-10).
- Source—Satan with God's permission (1:12; 2:6).
- Reason—testing and refining (1:6-12; 2:1-10; 23:10).
- Result—greater knowledge of God and understanding of self (42:1-6).
- Lesson—God and Satan may both be involved in the sending of our afflictions (Job 1:12; 2:6).

Miriam (Ex. 15:20-21; Num. 12; 26:59)

- Identity—sister of Moses and Aaron.
- Affliction—leprosy.
- Source—God.

- Reason—chastening for rebellion.
- Result—repentance, healing, restoration.
- Lesson—God sometimes uses suffering to chasten His disobedient children.

Ezekiel's Wife (Ezek. 24:15-27)

- Identity—wife of a major prophet.
- Affliction—her illness and death.
- Source—God.
- Reason—to illustrate God's dealings with the nation of Israel.
- Result—God was glorified (implied).
- Lesson—God sometimes uses suffering and even death to accomplish His purposes.

Mephibosheth (2 Sam. 4:4; 9:1-13)

- Identity—young grandson of King Saul.
- Affliction—crippled through a fall.
- Source—not given.
- Reason—not given.
- Result—lifetime affliction with no cure provided.
- Lesson—God doesn't always tell us the reason for our suffering.

Paul (2 Cor. 12:1-10)

- Identity—the great apostle to the Gentiles.
- Affliction—a thorn in the flesh (an unidentified physical malady).
- Source—a gift from God (implied) and a "messenger of Satan."
- Reason—to keep Paul from exalting himself because of his unique spiritual experiences.
- Result—the thorn remained with Paul in spite of his prayers for deliverance but became a blessing because it increased his dependence on the Lord.
- Lesson—God doesn't always bring temporal healing, even to His most devoted children.

Questions On Healing

In the following pages we will attempt to answer some common questions about healing that are often raised concerning certain biblical passages.

What about our authority to heal? In an *Our Daily Bread* article, I said that though we don't have the authority to call people back from death we can do practical things to help those who are sorrowing. Much to my surprise, several people wrote me, accusing me of not believing Matthew 10:7-8, "As you go, preach, saying, 'The kingdom of heaven is at hand.' Heal the sick, cleanse the lepers, raise the dead, cast out demons. Freely you have received, freely give."

Yes, the Lord gave His disciples authority to heal, perhaps even to raise the dead (although these words are not found in some of the early manuscript copies). But we err if we make these words our marching orders or view them as giving us authority to heal the sick and raise the dead. They were addressed to a small group of men who at that time, on the other side of Calvary, were preaching the "gospel of the kingdom" to Jews only. After referring to this passage, Dr. De Haan, in his inimitable way, wrote:

> They were not to accept money for their services; they were not to take any provision, but to live on the kindness and charity and generosity of the people to whom they ministered . . . . No lolling around in luxury for those apostles; no expensive hotel suites; but theirs was to be a life of rigor and self-denial; a life of poverty as became the followers of Him who had "nowhere to lay His head," who was born in a stable, depended on the charity of His friends, rode on a borrowed colt, and died on a sinner's cross. If, then, this commission in verse 8, "heal the sick," is to be taken for us today, it also should involve all of these other

instructions which the Lord gave in this connection. This verse is constantly quoted as a reason for the same miracles today, but surely consistency alone demands that the rest of the passage be made to apply as well.

What about healing in the atonement? "You need not be sick. Christ died for our sicknesses as well as our sins. Through faith we must claim freedom from illness just as we claim freedom from the penalty of our sins. That's what Matthew 8:16-17 tells us." A godly man dying of cancer heard a radio preacher say this. He became troubled. He began to suffer from a feeling of guilt about his lack of faith just as much as from his illness. I assured him that he had not failed spiritually. He and his loved ones had prayed earnestly. Neither their prayers nor their faith were deficient. It apparently was not God's will to heal him. The man was then able to face his approaching death with faith and courage.

> **Jesus' miracles of healing were signs of the complete healing that will be enjoyed ultimately by all who place their trust in Him.**

Let's examine Matthew 8:16-17 to see exactly what it says about the relationships between the atonement and healing. We read:

> When evening had come, they brought to Him many who were demon-possessed. And He cast out the spirits with a word, and healed all who were sick, that it might be fulfilled which was spoken by Isaiah the prophet, saying: "He Himself took our infirmities and bore our sicknesses."

The closing words are an accurate quotation from the Hebrew text of Isaiah 53:4. Jesus "took" our sicknesses by sympathetically and compassionately entering into the pains and sorrows of mankind. His miracles of healing were signs. They showed His compassion for us and pointed forward to His death by which He would pay the price for sin so that ultimately all suffering can end. His miracles of healing were signs of the complete healing that will be enjoyed ultimately by all who place their trust in Him.

Nothing in this passage even remotely suggests that we can claim physical healing through the atonement. D. A. Carson astutely observed, "The cross is the basis for all the benefits which accrue to believers; but this does not mean that all such benefits can be secured at the present time on demand, any more than we have the right and power to demand our resurrection bodies" (*The Expositor's Bible Commentary*, Vol. 8, Zondervan, p.267).

What about anointing services? In some church services, sick and suffering people are invited to come forward to be anointed with oil and prayed for. This practice is based on James 5:13-16. But the sick person in James calls for the elders to come to him. Perhaps he is too ill to go to them. The combination of the Greek word *asthenia* (sick) in verse 14 and *kamno* (sick) in verse 15 is seen by some Bible students as portraying someone who is flat in bed, probably hopelessly ill. This anointing does not occur in a public service or on invitation from the platform.

The elders are to pray for the sick person and anoint him with oil. This anointing with oil was ceremonial, not medicinal. Oil had no healing value for a person with a severe, life-threatening illness. Besides, James said that it is the "prayer of faith," not the oil, that saves the sick from physical death.

What is this prayer of faith? It certainly isn't a state of mind a person acquires through a lot of agonized crying or shouting. That goes against what Jesus said about praying (Mt. 6:7-15). The "prayer of faith" is Spirit-led praying that is sensitive to God's will and submissive to it.

James 5:13-16 was addressed to saints in the church age. But some Bible students believe that it was intended only for people who lived during the apostolic era. They point out that James was written at a very early date while the apostles who possessed the gifts of healings and discernment (1 Cor. 12:1-11) were still living. They also call our attention to the fact that the text seems to imply that healing could always be expected.

Many other Bible students, however, are not comfortable with this interpretation. They can't find solid reasons to limit this instruction to the apostolic era. They therefore say that we should honor requests for anointing and prayer from those who are ill. They also point out that confession of sin seems to be an important element in this anointing and prayer service.

Bible scholars do indeed differ as to the value of this practice in the church today. However, one thing is certain. No fair-minded person can make it the biblical basis for public anointing services.

What about the promise of John 14:12? Jesus told His disciples, "Most assuredly, I say to you, he who believes in Me, the works that I do he will do also; and greater works than these he will do, because I go to My Father" (Jn. 14:12). The first question we must ask ourselves is, "To whom was Jesus speaking?" The answer is clear: His disciples. Were His promises fulfilled? Yes, they were. Their miracles, some of which are recorded in Acts, were indeed similar to Christ's. But what about the "greater works"? They certainly weren't physical. How do you top feeding 5,000 people with a boy's lunch, calming a tempest with a word of command, and calling people back from death? The "greater works" undoubtedly refer to the spiritual triumphs of the gospel. The apostles, empowered by the Holy Spirit, led a movement that turned the world of their day upside down (Acts 17:6). Millions of people, mostly Gentiles, believed the good news and were transformed. In a period of just 30 years! Our Lord's promises to the apostles have been fulfilled.

Remember, our Lord was addressing His inner circle of disciples, and He fulfilled the promises He made to them. We have no right to take these words as a mandate for us to work miracles. Even during the time of the apostles the supernatural gifts of miracles and healing were sovereignly dispensed by God as He saw fit. He did not give the same gifts to all (1 Cor. 12:1-11). After listing the gifts, Paul wrote, "But one and the same Spirit works all these things, distributing to each one individually as He wills" (1 Cor. 12:11). Yes, God could choose to give us power to perform miracles like Jesus and the apostles. He is sovereign. But He didn't promise us miracle-working power. Not in John 14:12 or in any other Bible passage.

> **God could choose to give us power to perform miracles like Jesus and the apostles. But He didn't promise us miracle-working power.**

What about the gift of healing? Some Christian leaders are convinced that they possess the "gifts of healings" referred to in 1 Corinthians 12. Moreover, many sane, honest, and respectable people support this claim. They testify that they experienced or witnessed real healings through the laying on of hands in a healing service. And they challenge those who don't believe them to produce a New Testament verse that states explicitly that gifts of healings stopped with the apostles.

Now, it is true that the New Testament writers nowhere explicitly declare that the gifts of healings ceased. However, Hebrews 2:1-4 makes it clear that the miraculous sign gifts were not present in about AD 68 as they were at an earlier stage in the apostolic era. The writer of Hebrews declared that the message of salvation "was confirmed . . . both with signs and wonders, with various miracles, and gifts of the Holy Spirit, according to His own will" (Heb. 2:3-4). He used the past tense. In addition, he lumped together "signs and wonders" and "gifts of the Spirit." It appears that the supernatural sign gifts were no longer present to the extent that they were at an earlier time.

Present healings through prayer don't necessarily indicate that somebody exercised the gift of healing. God can heal in response to prayer whenever He chooses to do so.

Another matter of significance is the fact that in the Greek language, the supernatural sign gifts are written as double plurals—"gifts of healings," "gifts of tongues," "workings of miracles." This may indicate that the supernatural gifts did not reside in an individual like the gift of an office—apostle, prophet, evangelist, and pastor-teacher (Eph. 4:11). They apparently came upon a person for one event and had to be given again or renewed by the Holy Spirit according to His will. Perhaps that's why Paul, who on one occasion healed a host of people (Acts 19:11-12), couldn't heal Epaphroditus (Phil. 2:25-30), Trophimus (2 Tim. 4:20), or Timothy (1 Tim. 5:23).

Since even the apostles didn't possess a resident gift of healing, we have good reason to deny that anyone has it today. Then too, the recorded instances of miraculous healings during subsequent eras of church history should not be seen as evidence that the signs and wonders and gifts of healings continued. A divine healing need not be a sign or wonder, even if it is quite clearly supernatural. Nor do present healings through prayer indicate that somebody exercised the "gifts of healings." God can heal in response to prayer whenever He chooses to do so.

What about the astounding contemporary reports of healing? Wherever you go, you can find people who tell of being miraculously cured through prayer, through a visit to a shrine, or through the work of a healer. The tendency among non-Christians (and even many Christians) has been to disregard or deny these reports. Lately, however, many secularists are taking them more seriously without thinking of these unexplainable phenomena as divine miracles. They are quick to point out that spontaneous remissions and apparent healings occur among Christians and non-Christians. They find refuge in the mystery of the relationship between mind and matter and the unexplainable power of suggestion. They don't even attempt to refute testimonials of amazing healings by people who received treatment from quacks whose methods have no scientific validity.

> **We do not question the fact that God can and does heal. However, not all humanly unexplainable incidents are miracles of God.**

Our approach as Christians is different. We believe in God and His power to heal. Many of us have had firsthand experiences of amazing healings in response to prayer. Therefore, we do not question the fact that God can and does heal. However, we should recognize that not all humanly unexplainable incidents are miracles of God. They occur even among Satan worshipers! Therefore, we test a religious leader's credibility by what he teaches, not by an analysis of the miracles ascribed to him or her.

What about Paul's "thorn in the flesh"? In 2 Corinthians 12:1-10, Paul spoke of his "thorn in the flesh." He said that it was "given" him to keep him from becoming conceited because of the amazing revelations he had received. He also declared it to be "a messenger from Satan to buffet me." The giver of the thorn was undoubtedly God; He, not the devil, would be concerned to keep Paul humble. But Satan could use the thorn to distress him.

We don't know what the "thorn" was. A number of guesses have been made. Some have mentioned bad eyes, epilepsy, malaria. Others, eager to maintain that obedient Christians are free from disease, have mentioned an indwelling demon or bitter enemies. These last suggestions, however, don't fit Paul's words, "Therefore most gladly I will rather boast in my infirmities, that the power of Christ may rest upon me" (v.9). An indwelling demon or persistent enemies are not "weaknesses." The "thorn" was without question some kind of physical affliction. And God gave it to Paul for his spiritual good. God didn't remove it even though Paul prayed earnestly for its removal. But He provided such wonderful grace and strength that Paul saw it as a blessing.

The strength of our faith does not determine whether or not healing will come.

How much faith do I need? Many people have the idea that if we fulfill God's conditions by having enough faith, we will always be healed. Therefore they boldly "name and claim" complete healing when they pray. They even tell a person that he or she is well while the symptoms of the illness are still present.

Dr. Paul Brand in the November 25, 1983, issue of *Christianity Today* told the sad story about a family that took this approach. When their 15-month-old son came down with flu-like symptoms, they followed the advice of their church leaders and depended solely on prayer for his recovery. Their son kept getting more sick over the next several weeks, gradually losing his senses of hearing and sight. He finally died—and he remained dead in spite of fervent prayer that God would restore his life. The autopsy showed that the cause of death was a form of meningitis that could have been treated easily.

Now, these people had tremendous faith. But the strength of our faith does not determine whether or not healing will come. Some of our Lord's miracles were not in any way related to the faith of those who benefited from them (Mt. 12:9-13; Mk. 1:23-28; Lk. 7:11-15; 13:10-13; 14:1-6; 22:50-51; Jn. 9:1-38). Besides, are we going to say that Paul was not healed of his "thorn in the flesh" because he didn't have enough faith? Was Timothy's lack of faith the reason he had stomach problems? (1 Tim. 5:23).

Exploring The Scriptures

Isaiah 53:4—"Surely He has borne our griefs and carried our sorrows; yet we esteemed Him stricken, smitten by God, and afflicted."

Objective:
To examine and find biblical answers for issues on healing that can divide Christians.

Bible Memorization:
Isaiah 53:4

Reading:
"Sick And Suffering People In The Bible" & "Questions On Healing" pp.27-35

Warming Up

As you consider the questions on the preceding pages, it's hard to escape the reality of our passionate pursuit of physical well-being. Is it possible to be so concerned about our physical needs that we lose sight of our spiritual needs—and priorities? Defend your answer.

Thinking Through

On pages 27-28, we are given some biblical examples of people God didn't heal. Why were these godly individuals not healed?

On pages 29-35, we examined eight common questions about healing and looked at the Bible passages that are often quoted in connection with these issues. Do you agree with the author's answers to these questions? Are there any you disagree with? Which ones? Why?

We are warned on page 34 that sometimes even miracles can be deceptive works of Satan. Why would our spiritual enemy sometimes do good things? How could satanic acts that appear good undermine God's purposes for His children?

Digging In
Key Text: Hebrews 2:1-4

In verse 1, we are warned about the danger of drifting away. How is that drifting described? What is the cause of drifting? Its result?

According to verses 3 and 4, how did God "confirm" or "witness" to the great salvation He offered to mankind?

So, according to verse 4, what was the purpose of signs and wonders, with various miracles"? Do you think healing was one of these? What governs the use of the gifts of the Spirit?

"¹Therefore we must give the more earnest heed to the things we have heard, lest we drift away. ²For if the word spoken through angels proved steadfast, and every transgression and disobedience received a just reward, ³how shall we escape if we neglect so great a salvation, which at the first began to be spoken by the Lord, and was confirmed to us by those who heard Him, ⁴God also bearing witness both with signs and wonders, with various miracles, and gifts of the Holy Spirit, according to His own will?"

Going Further
Refer
Jesus often discouraged the publicizing of His healing miracles (Mt. 8:4; 9:30; 12:16; Mk. 7:36; Lk. 8:56). Why did Jesus prohibit such publicity? What does this say about today's highly publicized healing services?

Reflect
In light of this study on physical sickness, healing, and the control of God, we ultimately must face our need of spiritual healing that is found in God's great salvation (see p.40). Have you trusted Christ for the ultimate healing—the healing of sin and guilt through Jesus Christ? If not, will you do so now? If you have already trusted Christ for eternity, ask Him to help you trust Him for the trials of each day.

Hebrews 2:1-4

Does God Want Me Well?

We are now ready to answer directly the question that appears on the cover of this booklet. Yes, God wants you well—just as He "desires all men to be saved and to come to the knowledge of the truth" (1 Tim. 2:4). But not everyone accepts His offer of salvation. God would like to see His children well, but many of them disobey good health rules. Some fall into sinful ways and need to be chastened (Heb. 12:6). All of us are spiritually benefited by some trials and pain. Both Paul and James exhorted believers to be glad when they are tested by suffering (Rom. 5:3-5; Jas. 1:2-4). Their teachings assure us that it is an indispensable element in our spiritual development. God would like us well, but it would not be good for us to go through life without pain.

> **God's Word provides assurances**
> **and promotes a way of life that is conducive**
> **to physical and psychological wellness.**

It does not follow, however, that we should take a dim view of physical health or pleasure. Nor should we stoically resign ourselves to the idea that we should expect a lot of suffering. On the contrary, we should look at life optimistically. God's Word provides assurances and promotes a way of life that is conducive to physical and psychological wellness. It does so in at least nine ways:

1. It brings relief from the heavy burden of guilt (Ps. 32:1-2; Rom. 5:1).
2. It provides the power to release inner bitterness caused by an unforgiving spirit (Mt. 6:12,14-15; Eph. 4:32).

3. It promotes a positive view toward our body, assuring us that the Holy Spirit lives in it (1 Cor. 6:19), and that it is destined for resurrection (1 Cor. 15).
4. It teaches that sexual expression is both safe and satisfying within the bonds of marriage (1 Cor. 7:1-5; Heb. 13:4).
5. It provides grace for single believers, enabling them to live a happy and fulfilled life (1 Cor. 7:7-8,32,39-40).
6. It is marked by hope—a buoyant confidence about the future (Rom. 8:31-39).
7. It assures us that we are members of a select community—the body of Christ in which each person fills a special role for the mutual benefit of all (Rom. 12:3-8; 1 Cor. 12:1-31).
8. It fosters a unique relationship with God so that we can come to Him as our Father in an attitude of expectancy and ask Him for healing when we are sick (Mt. 7:7-11; Rom. 8:15; Jas. 5:14-15).
9. It enables us to rejoice even when we suffer pain (Acts 5:41; 2 Cor. 4:16-18).

God wants you well. He allows illness and pain only when He can use them for your good.

God wants you well. He allows illness and pain only when He can use them for your good. And He is going to see to it that you will be well for all eternity. Believing this will promote your good health.

Sickness, Healing, And You

The young seldom have personal contact with pain and sorrow. Grandparents are still alive for some. And even when they see these grandparents get sick or die, they can reason that it will be a long time before this happens to anybody in their immediate family. But sooner or later, everybody comes into close contact with pain, sorrow, and death. Therefore we should ask ourselves, "How will I cope when a doctor says, 'I'm sorry, we did all we could,' or 'I hope you are prepared for bad news. I must tell you that you have cancer, and that we can't do much for you.'"

If you have placed your trust in Jesus Christ, you can face such news calmly and hopefully. If you are not living obediently, you can turn away from your sin and back to God. You can ask the Lord for healing. You can pray with the absolute assurance that God will heal you if doing so will bring glory to Himself and further your eternal welfare. And if He doesn't make you well, He will give you His wonderful grace and use the affliction for good.

You can ask the Lord for healing.
You can pray with the absolute assurance
that God will heal you
if doing so will bring glory to Himself
and further your eternal welfare.

If you have never placed your trust in Jesus Christ, do it today. Acknowledge your sinfulness and your inability to save yourself. Believe that Jesus died on the cross for sinners and that He rose again. Then put your trust in Him. Believe that He did it for you. He will forgive you, make you a member of His family, and give you eternal life. He will take care of you through all time and eternity.

Discovery Series Bible Study Leader's And User's Guide

Statement Of Purpose

The *Discovery Series Bible Study* (DSBS) series provides assistance to pastors and leaders in discipling and teaching Christians through the use of RBC Ministries *Discovery Series* booklets. The DSBS series uses the inductive Bible-study method to help Christians understand the Bible more clearly.

Study Helps

Listed at the beginning of each study are the key verse, objective, and memorization verses. These will act as the compass and map for each study.

Some key Bible passages are printed out fully. This will help the students to focus on these passages and to examine and compare the Bible texts more easily—leading to a better understanding of their meanings. Serious students are encouraged to open their own Bible to examine the other Scriptures as well.

How To Use DSBS (for individuals and small groups)

Individuals—Personal Study
Read the designated pages of the book.
Carefully consider and answer all the questions.

Small Groups—Bible-Study Discussion
To maximize the value of the time spent together, each member should do the lesson work prior to the group meeting.
Recommended discussion time: 45–55 minutes.
Engage the group in a discussion of the questions, seeking full participation from each of the members.

Overview Of Lessons

Study	Topic	Bible Text	Reading	Questions
1	The Problem Of Pain Christians Agree And Disagree	2 Cor. 12:1-10	pp.4-7	pp.8-9
2	God Will Make You Well God Hurts When You Hurt	2 Cor. 4:16–5:1	pp.11-15	pp.16-17
3	God Knows Why You're Suffering God Is In Control	Jn. 9:1-5	pp.19-23	pp.24-25
4	Sick & Suffering People Questions On Healing	Heb. 2:1-4	pp.27-35	pp.36-37

The DSBS format incorporates a "layered" approach to Bible study that include four segments. These segments form a series of perspectives that becom increasingly more personalized and focused. These segments are:

Warming Up. In this section, a general interest question is used to begi the discussion (in small groups) or "to get the juices flowing" (in personal study). is intended to begin the process of interaction at the broadest, most general leve

Thinking Through. Here, the student or group is invited to intera with the *Discovery Series* material that has been read. In considering th information and implications of the booklet, these questions help to drive hom the critical concepts of that portion of the booklet.

Digging In. Moving away from the *Discovery Series* material, this sectio isolates a key biblical text from the manuscript and engages the student or grou in a brief inductive study of that passage of Scripture. This brings the authority c the Bible into the forefront of the study as we consider its message to our hear and lives.

Going Further. This final segment contains two parts. In *Refer,* th student or group has the opportunity to test the ideas of the lesson against th rest of the Bible by cross-referencing the text with other verses. In *Reflect,* th student or group is challenged to personally apply the lesson by making practical response to what has been learned.

Pulpit Sermon Series (for pastors and church leaders)

Although the *Discovery Series Bible Study* is primarily for personal and group study, pastors may want to use this material as the foundation for a series of messages on this important issue. The suggested topics and their corresponding texts are as follows:

Sermon No.	Topic	Text
1	Understanding The Problem	2 Cor. 12:1-10
2	Biblical Certainties (Pt. 1)	2 Cor. 4:16–5:1
3	Biblical Certainties (Pt. 2)	Jn. 9:1-5
4	Exploring The Scriptures	Heb. 2:1-4

Final Thoughts

The DSBS will provide an opportunity for growth and ministry. To internalize the spiritual truths of each study in a variety of environments, the material is arranged to allow for flexibility in the application of the truths discussed.

Whether DSBS is used in small-group Bible studies, adult Sunday school classes, adult Bible fellowships, men's and women's study groups, or church-wide applications, the key to the strength of the discussion will be found in the preparation of each participant. Likewise, the effectiveness of personal and pastoral use of this material will be directly related to the time committed to using this resource.

As you use, teach, or study this material, may you "grow in the grace and knowledge of our Lord and Savior Jesus Christ" (2 Pet. 3:18).

Reflections

OUR DAILY BREAD

Delivered right to your home!

What could be better than getting *Our Daily Bread?* How about having it delivered directly to your home?

You'll also have the opportunity to receive special offers or Bible-study booklets. And you'll get articles written on timely topics we all face, such as forgiveness and anger.

To order your copy of *Our Daily Bread,* write to us at:

USA: PO Box 2222, Grand Rapids, MI 49501-2222
CANADA: Box 1622, Windsor, ON N9A 6Z7
RBC Web site: www.odb.org/guide

Support for RBC Ministries comes from the gifts of our members and friends. We are not funded or endowed by any group or denomination.